ThiS BooK BudgeT PlanneR BelongS To

Name:-_____

Address:-_____

Phone:-_____

Email:-_____

BudgeT PlanneR

Expenses

Income		TOTAL
INCOME 1		
INCOME 2		
OTHER INCOME		
TOTALE INCOME		

MONTH	
BUDGET	

Bill To Be Paid	Date Due	Amount
Totale		

Monthly BudgeT PlanneR

Others Expenese	Date Due	Amount
Totale		

Totale Income		
Totale Expenses		
Difference		

Notes:- _

_ _

_ _

Weekly Expenses Traker

budget _____   Month _____   Week of _____

Monday Date:- _ _ _ _ _ _ _ _ _ _ _ _

Description	Amount
Total	

Weekly Expenses Traker

budget   Month   Week of

Monday Date:- _ _ _ _ _ _ _ _ _ _ _ _ _

Description	Amount
Total	

Weekly Expenses Traker

budget   Month   Week of

Monday Date:- _ _ _ _ _ _ _ _ _ _ _ _

Description	Amount
Total	

Weekly Expenses Traker

budget   Month   Week of

Tuesday Date:-_ _ _ _ _ _ _ _ _ _ _ _ _

Description	Amount
Total	

Weekly Expenses Traker

Budget _____ Month _____ Week of _____

Wednesday Date:- _ _ _ _ _ _ _ _ _ _ _ _

Description	Amount
Total	

Weekly Expenses Traker

Budget   Month   Week of

Thursday Date:- _ _ _ _ _ _ _ _ _ _ _ _

Description	Amount
Total	

Weekly Expenses Traker

Budget   Month   Week of

Friday Date:- _ _ _ _ _ _ _ _ _ _ _

Description	Amount
Total	

Weekly Expenses Traker

Budget   Month   Week of

Saturday Date:-_ _ _ _ _ _ _ _ _ _ _ _ _

Description	Amount
Total	

Weekly Expenses Traker

Budget   Month   Week of

Sunday Date:- _ _ _ _ _ _ _ _ _ _ _

Description	Amount
Total	

BudgeT PlanneR

Expenses

Income		TOTAL
INCOME 1		
INCOME 2		
OTHER INCOME		
TOTALE INCOME		

MONTH	
BUDGET	

Bill To Be Paid	Date Due	Amount
Totale		

Monthly BudgeT PlanneR

Others Expenese	Date Due	Amount
Totale		

Totale Income		
Totale Expenses		
Difference		

Notes:- _

_ _

_ _

Weekly Expenses Traker

budget   Month   Week of

Monday Date:- _ _ _ _ _ _ _ _ _ _ _

Description	Amount
Total	

Weekly Expenses Traker

budget   Month   Week of

Tuesday Date:- _ _ _ _ _ _ _ _ _ _ _ _

Description	Amount
Total	

Weekly Expenses Traker

Budget   Month   Week of

Wednesday Date:- _ _ _ _ _ _ _ _ _ _

Description	Amount
Total	

Weekly Expenses Traker

Budget   Month   Week of

Thursday Date:- _ _ _ _ _ _ _ _ _ _ _ _ _

Description	Amount
Total	

Weekly Expenses Traker

Budget   Month   Week of

Friday Date:- _ _ _ _ _ _ _ _ _ _ _ _

Description	Amount
Total	

Weekly Expenses Traker

Budget _____   Month _____   Week of _____

Saturday Date:- _ _ _ _ _ _ _ _ _ _ _ _ _

Description	Amount
Total	

Weekly Expenses Traker

Budget   Month   Week of

Sunday Date:- _ _ _ _ _ _ _ _ _ _ _ _ _

Description	Amount
Total	

BudgeT PlanneR

Expenses

Income		TOTAL
INCOME 1		
INCOME 2		
OTHER INCOME		
TOTALE INCOME		

MONTH	
BUDGET	

Bill To Be Paid	Date Due	Amount
Totale		

Monthly BudgeT PlanneR

Others Expenese	Date Due	Amount
Totale		

Totale Income		
Totale Expenses		
Difference		

Notes:- _____

_____

_____

Weekly Expenses Traker

budget   Month   Week of

Monday Date:- _ _ _ _ _ _ _ _ _ _ _ _ _

Description	Amount
Total	

Weekly Expenses Traker

budget   Month   Week of

Tuesday Date:-_ _ _ _ _ _ _ _ _ _ _ _

Description	Amount
Total	

Weekly Expenses Traker

Budget   Month   Week of

Wednesday Date:- _ _ _ _ _ _ _ _ _ _

Description	Amount
Total	

Weekly Expenses Traker

Budget   Month   Week of

Thursday Date:- _ _ _ _ _ _ _ _ _

Description	Amount
Total	

Weekly Expenses Traker

Budget   Month   Week of

Friday Date:- _ _ _ _ _ _ _ _ _ _ _ _

Description	Amount
Total	

Weekly Expenses Traker

Budget   Month   Week of

Saturday Date:-_ _ _ _ _ _ _ _ _ _ _ _

Description	Amount
Total	

Weekly Expenses Traker

Budget   Month   Week of

Sunday Date:- _ _ _ _ _ _ _ _ _ _ _

Description	Amount
Total	

BudgeT PlanneR

Expenses

Income		TOTAL
INCOME 1		
INCOME 2		
OTHER INCOME		
TOTALE INCOME		

MONTH	
BUDGET	

Bill To Be Paid	Date Due	Amount
Totale		

Monthly BudgeT PlanneR

Others Expenese	Date Due	Amount
Totale		

Totale Income		
Totale Expenses		
Difference		

Notes:- _____

_____

_____

Weekly Expenses Traker

budget   Month   Week of

Monday Date:- _ _ _ _ _ _ _ _ _ _ _ _ _

Description	Amount
Total	

Weekly Expenses Traker

budget   Month   Week of

Tuesday Date:- _ _ _ _ _ _ _ _ _ _ _

Description	Amount
Total	

Weekly Expenses Traker

Budget   Month   Week of

Wednesday Date:- _ _ _ _ _ _ _ _ _ _

Description	Amount
Total	

Weekly Expenses Traker

Budget   Month   Week of

Thursday Date:-_ _ _ _ _ _ _ _ _ _ _ _

Description	Amount
Total	

Weekly Expenses Traker

Budget   Month   Week of

Friday Date:- _ _ _ _ _ _ _ _ _ _ _ _

Description	Amount
Total	

Weekly Expenses Traker

Budget   Month   Week of

Saturday Date:-_ _ _ _ _ _ _ _ _ _ _

Description	Amount
Total	

Weekly Expenses Traker

Budget   Month   Week of

Sunday Date:- _ _ _ _ _ _ _ _ _ _ _ _

Description	Amount
Total	

BudgeT PlanneR

Expenses

Income		TOTAL
INCOME 1		
INCOME 2		
OTHER INCOME		
TOTALE INCOME		

MONTH	
BUDGET	

Bill To Be Paid	Date Due	Amount
Totale		

Monthly BudgeT PlanneR

Others Expenese	Date Due	Amount
Totale		

Totale Income		
Totale Expenses		
Difference		

Notes:- _____

_____

_____

Weekly Expenses Traker

budget   Month   Week of

Monday Date:- _ _ _ _ _ _ _ _ _ _ _ _

Description	Amount
Total	

Weekly Expenses Traker

budget   Month   Week of

Tuesday Date:-_ _ _ _ _ _ _ _ _ _ _

Description	Amount
Total	

Weekly Expenses Traker

Budget   Month   Week of

Wednesday Date:-_ _ _ _ _ _ _ _ _ _

Description	Amount
Total	

Weekly Expenses Traker

Budget   Month   Week of

Thursday Date:- _ _ _ _ _ _ _ _ _ _ _ _

Description	Amount
Total	

Weekly Expenses Traker

Budget   Month   Week of

Friday Date:- _ _ _ _ _ _ _ _ _ _ _

Description	Amount
Total	

Weekly Expenses Traker

Budget   Month   Week of

Saturday Date:-_ _ _ _ _ _ _ _ _ _ _ _ _ _

Description	Amount
Total	

Weekly Expenses Traker

Budget   Month   Week of

Sunday Date:- _ _ _ _ _ _ _ _ _ _ _ _

Description	Amount
Total	

BudgeT PlanneR

Expenses

Income		TOTAL
INCOME 1		
INCOME 2		
OTHER INCOME		
TOTALE INCOME		

MONTH	
BUDGET	

Bill To Be Paid	Date Due	Amount
Totale		

Monthly BudgeT PlanneR

Others Expenese	Date Due	Amount
Totale		

Totale Income		
Totale Expenses		
Difference		

Notes:- _

_ _

_ _

Weekly Expenses Traker

budget   Month   Week of

Monday Date:- _ _ _ _ _ _ _ _ _ _ _

Description	Amount
Total	

Weekly Expenses Traker

budget   Month   Week of

Tuesday Date:- _ _ _ _ _ _ _ _ _ _ _

Description	Amount
Total	

Weekly Expenses Traker

Budget   Month   Week of

Wednesday Date:- _ _ _ _ _ _ _ _ _ _ _

Description	Amount
Total	

Weekly Expenses Traker

Budget   Month   Week of

Thursday Date:- _ _ _ _ _ _ _ _ _ _ _

Description	Amount
Total	

Weekly Expenses Traker

Budget   Month   Week of

Friday Date:- _ _ _ _ _ _ _ _ _ _ _ _ _

Description	Amount
Total	

Weekly Expenses Traker

Budget   Month   Week of

Saturday Date:-_ _ _ _ _ _ _ _ _ _ _

Description	Amount
Total	

Weekly Expenses Traker

Budget   Month   Week of

Sunday Date:- _ _ _ _ _ _ _ _ _ _ _ _ _

Description	Amount
Total	

Budget Planner

Expenses

Income		TOTAL
INCOME 1		
INCOME 2		
OTHER INCOME		
TOTALE INCOME		

MONTH	
BUDGET	

Bill To Be Paid	Date Due	Amount
Totale		

Monthly BudgeT PlanneR

Others Expenese	Date Due	Amount
Totale		

Totale Income		
Totale Expenses		
Difference		

Notes:- _____

_____

_____

Weekly Expenses Traker

budget   Month   Week of

Monday Date:- _ _ _ _ _ _ _ _ _ _ _ _

Description	Amount
Total	

Weekly Expenses Traker

budget   Month   Week of

Tuesday Date:- _ _ _ _ _ _ _ _ _ _ _ _ _

Description	Amount
Total	

Weekly Expenses Traker

Budget   Month   Week of

Wednesday Date:- _ _ _ _ _ _ _ _ _ _

Description	Amount
Total	

Weekly Expenses Traker

Budget   Month   Week of

Thursday Date:- _ _ _ _ _ _ _ _ _ _ _ _

Description	Amount
Total	

Weekly Expenses Traker

Budget   Month   Week of

Friday Date:- _ _ _ _ _ _ _ _ _ _ _

Description	Amount
Total	

Weekly Expenses Traker

Budget   Month   Week of

Saturday Date:-_ _ _ _ _ _ _ _ _ _ _ _

Description	Amount
Total	

Weekly Expenses Traker

Budget   Month   Week of

Sunday Date:- _ _ _ _ _ _ _ _ _ _ _

Description	Amount
Total	

BudgeT PlanneR

Income		TOTAL
INCOME 1		
INCOME 2		
OTHER INCOME		
TOTALE INCOME		

Expenses

MONTH	
BUDGET	

Bill To Be Paid	Date Due	Amount
Totale		

Monthly BudgeT PlanneR

Others Expenese	Date Due	Amount
Totale		

Totale Income		
Totale Expenses		
Difference		

Notes:- _____

_____

_____

Weekly Expenses Traker

budget   Month   Week of

Monday Date:- _ _ _ _ _ _ _ _ _ _ _ _ _ _

Description	Amount
Total	

Weekly Expenses Traker

budget   Month   Week of

Tuesday Date:-_ _ _ _ _ _ _ _ _ _ _ _ _

Description	Amount
Total	

Weekly Expenses Traker

Budget   Month   Week of

Wednesday Date:- _ _ _ _ _ _ _ _ _ _

Description	Amount
Total	

Weekly Expenses Traker

Budget   Month   Week of

Thursday Date:- _ _ _ _ _ _ _ _ _ _

Description	Amount
Total	

Weekly Expenses Traker

Budget   Month   Week of

Friday Date:- _ _ _ _ _ _ _ _ _ _ _

Description	Amount
Total	

Weekly Expenses Traker

Budget	Month	Week of

Saturday Date:-_ _ _ _ _ _ _ _ _ _ _ _

Description	Amount
Total	

Weekly Expenses Traker

Budget   Month   Week of

Sunday Date:- _ _ _ _ _ _ _ _ _ _ _ _

Description	Amount
Total	

BudgeT PlanneR

Expenses

Income	TOTAL
INCOME 1	
INCOME 2	
OTHER INCOME	
TOTALE INCOME	

MONTH	
BUDGET	

Bill To Be Paid	Date Due	Amount
Totale		

Monthly BudgeT PlanneR

Others Expenese	Date Due	Amount
Totale		

Totale Income		
Totale Expenses		
Difference		

Notes:- _

_ _

_ _

Weekly Expenses Traker

budget   Month   Week of

Monday Date:- _ _ _ _ _ _ _ _ _ _ _

Description	Amount
Total	

Weekly Expenses Traker

budget   Month   Week of

Tuesday Date:-_ _ _ _ _ _ _ _ _ _ _ _ _ _ _

Description	Amount
Total	

Weekly Expenses Traker

Budget   Month   Week of

Wednesday Date:- _ _ _ _ _ _ _ _ _ _

Description	Amount
Total	

Weekly Expenses Traker

Budget   Month   Week of

Thursday Date:- _ _ _ _ _ _ _ _ _ _

Description	Amount
Total	

Weekly Expenses Traker

Budget   Month   Week of

Friday Date:- _ _ _ _ _ _ _ _ _ _ _ _

Description	Amount
Total	

Weekly Expenses Traker

Budget   Month   Week of

Saturday Date:-_ _ _ _ _ _ _ _ _ _ _ _ _ _

Description	Amount
Total	

Weekly Expenses Traker

Budget   Month   Week of

Sunday Date:- _ _ _ _ _ _ _ _ _ _ _

Description	Amount
Total	

BudgeT PlanneR

Expenses

Income		TOTAL
INCOME 1		
INCOME 2		
OTHER INCOME		
TOTALE INCOME		

MONTH	
BUDGET	

Bill To Be Paid	Date Due	Amount
Totale		

Monthly BudgeT PlanneR

Others Expenese	Date Due	Amount
Totale		

Totale Income		
Totale Expenses		
Difference		

Notes:- _

_ _

_ _

Weekly Expenses Traker

budget   Month   Week of

Monday Date:- _ _ _ _ _ _ _ _ _ _ _

Description	Amount
Total	

Weekly Expenses Traker

budget   Month   Week of

Tuesday Date:- _ _ _ _ _ _ _ _ _ _ _ _

Description	Amount
Total	

Weekly Expenses Traken

Budget   Month   Week of

Wednesday Date:- _ _ _ _ _ _ _ _ _ _

Description	Amount
Total	

Weekly Expenses Traker

Budget   Month   Week of

Thursday Date:- _ _ _ _ _ _ _ _ _ _ _ _

Description	Amount
Total	

Weekly Expenses Traker

Budget   Month   Week of

Friday Date:- _ _ _ _ _ _ _ _ _ _ _

Description	Amount
Total	

Weekly Expenses Traker

Budget   Month   Week of

Saturday Date:-_ _ _ _ _ _ _ _ _ _ _ _

Description	Amount
Total	

Weekly Expenses Traker

Budget   Month   Week of

Sunday Date:- _ _ _ _ _ _ _ _ _ _ _ _

Description	Amount
Total	

Budget Planner

Income		TOTAL
INCOME 1		
INCOME 2		
OTHER INCOME		
TOTALE INCOME		

Expenses

MONTH	
BUDGET	

Bill To Be Paid	Date Due	Amount
Totale		

Monthly BudgeT PlanneR

Others Expenese	Date Due	Amount
Totale		

Totale Income		
Totale Expenses		
Difference		

Notes:- _

_ _

_ _

Weekly Expenses Traker

budget   Month   Week of

Monday Date:- _ _ _ _ _ _ _ _ _ _ _ _

Description	Amount
Total	

Weekly Expenses Traker

budget   Month   Week of

Tuesday Date:-_ _ _ _ _ _ _ _ _ _ _ _ _

Description	Amount
Total	

Weekly Expenses Traker

Budget   Month   Week of

Wednesday Date:- _ _ _ _ _ _ _ _ _ _

Description	Amount
Total	

Weekly Expenses Traker

Budget   Month   Week of

Thursday Date:- _ _ _ _ _ _ _ _ _ _ _ _

Description	Amount
Total	

Weekly Expenses Traker

Budget   Month   Week of

Friday Date:- _ _ _ _ _ _ _ _ _ _ _ _

Description	Amount
Total	

Weekly Expenses Traker

Budget   Month   Week of

Saturday Date:-_ _ _ _ _ _ _ _ _ _ _ _ _

Description	Amount
Total	

Weekly Expenses Traker

Budget   Month   Week of

Sunday Date:- _ _ _ _ _ _ _ _ _ _ _ _ _

Description	Amount
Total	

Budget Planner

Expenses

Income		TOTAL
INCOME 1		
INCOME 2		
OTHER INCOME		
TOTALE INCOME		

MONTH	
BUDGET	

Bill To Be Paid	Date Due	Amount
Totale		

Monthly BudgeT PlanneR

Others Expenese	Date Due	Amount
Totale		

Totale Income		
Totale Expenses		
Difference		

Notes:- _

_ _

_ _

Weekly Expenses Traker

budget   Month   Week of

Monday Date:- _ _ _ _ _ _ _ _ _ _ _

Description	Amount
Total	

Weekly Expenses Traker

budget   Month   Week of

Tuesday Date:- _ _ _ _ _ _ _ _ _ _ _ _

Description	Amount
Total	

Weekly Expenses Traker

Budget   Month   Week of

Wednesday Date:- _ _ _ _ _ _ _ _ _ _

Description	Amount
Total	

Weekly Expenses Traker

Budget   Month   Week of

Thursday Date:- _ _ _ _ _ _ _ _ _ _ _

Description	Amount
Total	

Weekly Expenses Traker

Budget   Month   Week of

Friday Date:- _ _ _ _ _ _ _ _ _ _ _ _

Description	Amount
Total	

Weekly Expenses Traker

Budget   Month   Week of

Saturday Date:-_ _ _ _ _ _ _ _ _ _ _ _ _

Description	Amount
Total	

Weekly Expenses Traker

Budget   Month   Week of

Sunday Date:- _ _ _ _ _ _ _ _ _ _ _

Description	Amount
Total	

BudgeT PlanneR

Expenses

Income		TOTAL
INCOME 1		
INCOME 2		
OTHER INCOME		
TOTALE INCOME		

MONTH	
BUDGET	

Bill To Be Paid	Date Due	Amount
Totale		

Monthly BudgeT PlanneR

Others Expenese	Date Due	Amount
Totale		

Totale Income		
Totale Expenses		
Difference		

Notes:- _

_ _

_ _

Weekly Expenses Traker

budget   Month   Week of

Monday Date:- _ _ _ _ _ _ _ _ _ _ _ _ _

Description	Amount
Total	

Weekly Expenses Traker

budget   Month   Week of

Tuesday Date:-_ _ _ _ _ _ _ _ _ _ _ _ _

Description	Amount
Total	

Weekly Expenses Traker

Budget   Month   Week of

Wednesday Date:- _ _ _ _ _ _ _ _ _ _

Description	Amount
Total	

Weekly Expenses Traker

Budget   Month   Week of

Thursday Date:- _ _ _ _ _ _ _ _ _ _ _ _ _

Description	Amount
Total	

Weekly Expenses Traker

Budget   Month   Week of

Friday Date:- _ _ _ _ _ _ _ _ _ _ _ _

Description	Amount
Total	

Weekly Expenses Traker

Budget   Month   Week of

Saturday Date:-_ _ _ _ _ _ _ _ _ _ _ _ _

Description	Amount
Total	

Weekly Expenses Traker

Budget   Month   Week of

Sunday Date:- _ _ _ _ _ _ _ _ _ _ _ _ _

Description	Amount
Total	

BudgeT PlanneR

Expenses

Income		TOTAL
INCOME 1		
INCOME 2		
OTHER INCOME		
TOTALE INCOME		

MONTH	
BUDGET	

Bill To Be Paid	Date Due	Amount
Totale		

Monthly BudgeT PlanneR

Others Expenese	Date Due	Amount
Totale		

Totale Income		
Totale Expenses		
Difference		

Notes:- _

_ _

_ _

Weekly Expenses Traker

budget   Month   Week of

Monday Date:- _ _ _ _ _ _ _ _ _ _ _ _ _ _ _

Description	Amount
Total	

Weekly Expenses Traker

budget   Month   Week of

Tuesday Date:- _ _ _ _ _ _ _ _ _ _ _ _

Description	Amount
Total	

Weekly Expenses Traker

Budget   Month   Week of

Wednesday Date:- _ _ _ _ _ _ _ _ _ _ _ _

Description	Amount
Total	

Weekly Expenses Traker

Budget   Month   Week of

Thursday Date:- _ _ _ _ _ _ _ _ _ _

Description	Amount
Total	

Weekly Expenses Traker

Budget   Month   Week of

Friday Date:- _ _ _ _ _ _ _ _ _ _ _ _

Description	Amount
Total	

Weekly Expenses Traker

Budget   Month   Week of

Saturday Date:-_ _ _ _ _ _ _ _ _ _ _ _

Description	Amount
Total	

Weekly Expenses Traker

Budget   Month   Week of

Sunday Date:- _ _ _ _ _ _ _ _ _ _ _ _ _

Description	Amount
Total	

BudgeT PlanneR

Expenses

Income		TOTAL
INCOME 1		
INCOME 2		
OTHER INCOME		
TOTALE INCOME		

MONTH	
BUDGET	

Bill To Be Paid	Date Due	Amount
Totale		

Made in United States
Troutdale, OR
01/09/2024